SO-BTD-814

DATE DUE

NOV 4 1982			
staff			
MAY 1 3 1989			
MAY 0 6 1991			
NOV 0 9 1995			
3-6-97 : IL			
APR 0 5 1997			
DEC 1 6 1999			
DEC 0 7 2004			

DEMCO 38-297

RENNER LEARNING RESOURCE CENTER
ELGIN COMMUNITY COLLEGE
ELGIN, ILLINOIS 60120

The Best of Rube Goldberg

RENNER LEARNING RESOURCE CENTER
ELGIN COMMUNITY COLLEGE
ELGIN, ILLINOIS

THE BEST OF RUBE GOLDBERG

compiled by CHARLES KELLER

Prentice-Hall Inc. | Englewood Cliffs, New Jersey

Copyright © 1914, 1915, 1916, 1919, 1920, 1921,
1922, 1923, 1924, 1926, 1927, 1928, 1929, 1930,
1931, 1939, 1944 by Rube Goldberg, (permission
granted by King Features Syndicate, Inc.)

All rights reserved. No part of this book may be
reproduced in any form or by any means, except for
the inclusion of brief quotations in a review,
without permission in writing from the publisher.
Printed in the United States of America   J

Prentice-Hall International, Inc., London
Prentice-Hall of Australia, Pty. Ltd., North Sydney
Prentice-Hall of Canada, Ltd., Toronto
Prentice-Hall of India Private Ltd., New Delhi
Prentice-Hall of Japan, Inc., Tokyo
Prentice-Hall of Southeast Asia Pte. Ltd., Singapore
Whitehall Books Limited, Wellington, New Zealand

   2   3   4   5   6   7   8   9   10

Library of Congress Cataloging in Publication Data
Goldberg, Reuben Lucius, 1883-1970.
   The best of Rube Goldberg.

   SUMMARY: A collection of more than 90 humorous
inventions which have appeared in the author's cartoons
during his career.
   1. Inventions—Caricatures and cartoons—Juvenile
literature.   2. American wit and humor, Pictorial—
Juvenile literature.   [1. Inventions—Caricatures and
cartoons.   2. Wit and humor]   I. Keller, Charles.
II. Title.
NC1429.G46A4   1979   741.5'973   79-15180
ISBN 0-13-074807-2
ISBN 0-13-074799-8 pbk.

To Louisa and Carl

Contents

Introduction

Americans have always been interested in a better mousetrap. Gadgets fascinate us. No one in America has expressed this fascination better than Reuben Lucius Goldberg, known as Rube Goldberg. For 55 years, from the period during World War I to his death in 1970, the award-winning cartoonist kept drawing machines and contraptions of marvelous complexity and ingenuity to perform such basic tasks as scratching your back or killing a mosquito. His cartoons took 20th-century machines back into the Stone Age.

Today Rube Goldberg is increasingly recognized as one of America's most popular cartoonists and a leading humorist of the early machine age. His inventions stand as commentaries on our age. They seize our interest with their clever and elaborately constructed designs while at the same time making us chuckle at our own mania for machinery. Our disproportionate reliance on gadgets might just border on the ridiculous, and Goldberg's understanding of this was original.

During his life, Rube Goldberg's drawings included sports cartoons, comic strips, and political cartoons. But his enduring contribution to comic art were his cartoons of inventions, some of which are coming to be regarded as comic masterpieces. While most machines work to make difficult tasks simple, his inventions made simple tasks howlingly complex. Dozens of arms, wheels, gears, handles, cups, and rods were set going aided by basketballs, canary cages, pails, boots, bathtubs, paddles, and live animals, to slice an orange or close a window if it starts raining while you are away from your house. The directions for working these gadgets were as simple as instructions for assembling a child's toy. We marvel—and we smile—at people's follies, and our own readiness to be taken in.

Goldberg's drawings of absurdly connected machines that actually seemed to work became so widely known that Webster's Dictionary added "rube goldberg" to its listing, defining it as "accomplishing by extremely complex, roundabout means what seemingly could be done simply." His name has become associated with any screwball apparatus that performs a simple task. We have all watched in fascination before some "Rube Goldberg" contraption.

Each Goldberg invention is an intricate play with objects, animals, and people interacting in a chain reaction to accomplish a trivial yet important job, like scratching one's back. The series of causes and effects is entirely—or almost entirely—plausible. The chain of unlikely events proceeds to its conclusion with believable logic. The ridiculous machine, to our amusement, works.

Goldberg's inventions discovered a harder way to achieve easy results. In their inventor's words they were, "symbols of man's capacity for exerting maximum effort to accomplish minimal results." He believed that there are two ways to do things, the simple way and the hard way, and that a surprisingly large number of people preferred doing it the hard way.

Rube Goldberg was born in 1883 in San Francisco. His father, a practical man, insisted he go to college to become a mining engineer, an education he later used for a peculiar form of engineering. But Goldberg loved to draw and got a job instead as a sports cartoonist for the San Francisco Chronicle newspaper. He soon moved to New York to do daily cartoons for the New York Evening Mail. One day in 1914 he drew a weird cartoon of a complicated machine that purported to help people lose weight. It struck people as both insane and logical—and wonderfully amusing. Before long Goldberg was doing mechanical drawings on a regular basis. They were immensely popular.

By 1928 Goldberg's cartoons were nationally syndicated and printed in newspapers all around the country and he was earning a phenomenal $125,000 a year. He also wrote occasional articles and stories for magazines and even traveled as a vaudeville act with Goldberg drawing funny cartoons swiftly on stage. Later in his life he drew political cartoons, one of which, about the terrible dilemma of atomic power, won a Pulitzer Prize in 1948. He also worked, in later life, to become a serious sculptor.

But it is his mechanical inventions that have charmed, fascinated, and amused people. Like the comic strips which grew up alongside his own work, and which Goldberg also drew for a time, Goldberg's work merged commercial art and humor in an original way that amounted to a new American art form.

Goldberg's inventions satirized the machine age around him and the spread of needless gadgetry. Yet, because his drawings were ingeniously arranged, logical, and almost believable, they fascinated Americans. And, because his work was gentle and full of humor, Goldberg's cartoons were thought of as more screwball than satire.

Rube Goldberg's work will endure because he gave priority to simple human needs and treasured basic human values. He was skeptical about advanced technology and big science, which contributed to making his own mechanical inventions primitive and full of human and animal parts. In our day, when we have begun to discard some of the more frivolous and wasteful of our gadgets, to conserve energy, and question the worth of too much technology and expensive machinery, Goldberg begins to seem like a prophet.

I have tried to select the best of Rube Goldberg's inventions and let them stand without further comment. Perhaps one or two may even help you or cause you to reconsider the manner in which you perform some of the commonplace tasks we all do.

Automatic Weight-Reducing Machine

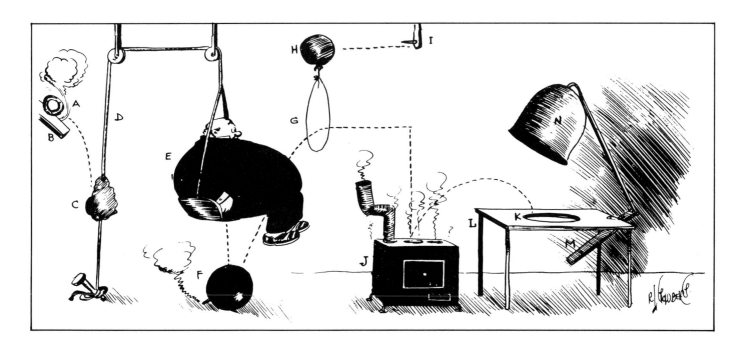

Doughnut (**A**) rolls down board (**B**) and becomes overheated from friction–hot doughnut falls on lump of wax (**C**), melting it and parting rope (**D**) releasing fat man (**E**) who falls on bomb (**F**)–bomb explodes, blowing man threw loop (**G**) suspended from balloon (**H**)–balloon moves in horizontal direction and bumps into pin (**I**) which punctures it, dropping subject on red-hot stove (**J**)–he naturally rises hurriedly to table (**L**) and falls into hole (**K**)–he hits lever (**M**), bringing bell (**N**) down tightly over his body–he cannot pass through hole and cannot call for help because bell is sound-proof–so he remains without food until body is thin enough to pass through hole.

Lighting a Cigar in an Automobile Doing Fifty Miles Per Hour

When automobile speeds at fifty miles an hour motorcycle cop (**A**) starts in pursuit–motorcycle hits cat (**B**), causing it to fall on button (**C**) which sets off cannon (**D**)–cannon ball (**E**) hits ivory dome of barber (**F**), bouncing off and knocking neck off bottle of strong acid (**G**)–acid drops on gold nugget (**H**), dissolving it–weight of kernels of corn (**J**) lower board (**I**) and fall into flower pot (**K**)–corn grows till it reaches height (**L**)–can of lima beans (**M**) jumps at corn on account of the natural affinity for succotash–string on end of can pulls lever (**O**) which pushes pointer (**P**) into paper tank (**Q**) half filled with water in which sardine (**R**) is swimming–pointer punctures paper tank, water runs out and sardine catches severe cold from exposure–sardine contracts a very high fever that finally sets fire to paper tank and lights cigar (**S**).

Hiding a Gravy Spot on Your Vest

Cheese (**A**), after standing around for several weeks, grows restless and falls off platform (**B**), hitting spring (**C**) and bouncing against electric button (**D**) which releases arrow held by mechanical cupid (**E**)–arrow cuts string (**F**), dropping weight (**G**) into bucket of water (**H**)–water splashes on tramp (**I**) who faints from the shock and drops against boomerang-throwing machine (**J**)–boomerang (**K**) shoots all over the place and finally strikes end of fountain pen (**L**), knocking ink-blot on paper (**M**)–eraser-hound (**N**) jumps at paper to rub out ink-blot with his nose–string (**O**) sets off aeroplane gun (**P**)–bullet (**Q**) hits board (**R**) which squeezes bulbs on end of droppers (**S**)–droppers contain ink the same color as the gravy spot–the ink drops fall all over vest making it impossible to tell which one of the spots is gravy–and you have a fancy vest in the bargain.

Simple Alarm Clock

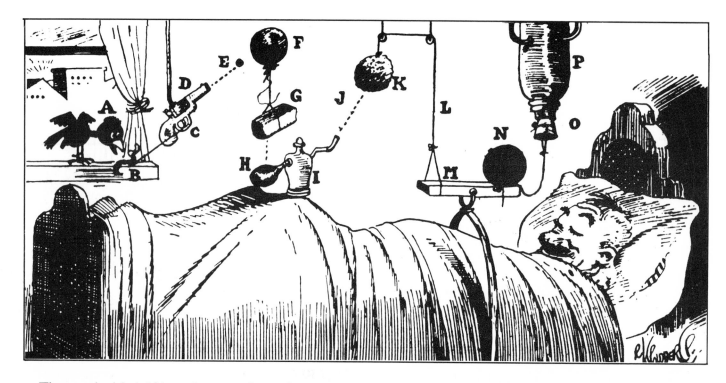

The early bird (**A**) arrives and catches worm (**B**), pulling string (**C**) and shooting off pistol (**D**). Bullet (**E**) busts balloon (**F**), dropping brick (**G**) on bulb (**H**) of atomizer (**I**) and shooting perfume (**J**) on sponge (**K**)–As sponge gains in weight, it lowers itself and pulls string (**L**), raising end of board (**M**)–Cannon ball (**N**) drops on nose of sleeping gentleman–String tied to cannon ball releases cork (**O**) of vacuum bottle (**P**) and ice water falls on sleeper's face to assist the cannon ball in its good work.

Simple Way to Mix Your Own Drinks at Home

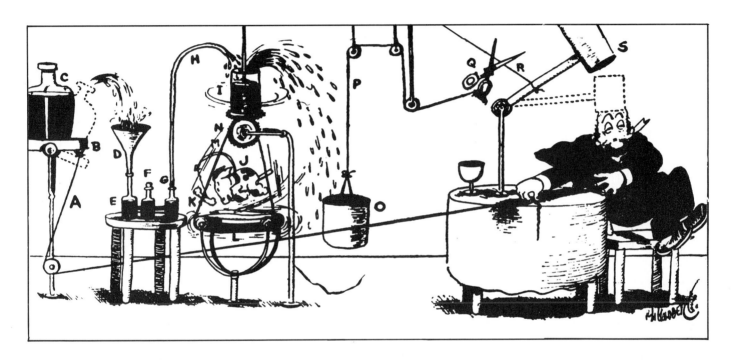

Take seat at table and pull string (**A**) tilting platform (**B**) causing wood alcohol (**C**) to fall in funnel (**D**)–Wood-alcohol mixes with furniture polish, bay rum and coal oil in bottles (**E,F,G**) and is forced up through tube (**H**) into glass (**I**)–Dog (**J**) chases bone (**K**), turning treadmill (**L**) connected with pulley (**M**) to cog-wheel (**N**) which mixes drink in glass–Mixture is too poisonous to drink–so revolution of glass causes fluid to fall in tank (**O**)–The weight pulls string (**P**) causing scissors (**Q**) to cut thread (**R**), letting hammer (**S**) fall on your head, giving same effect as harmless, old-fashioned souse!

Keep the Baby From Disturbing You at Night

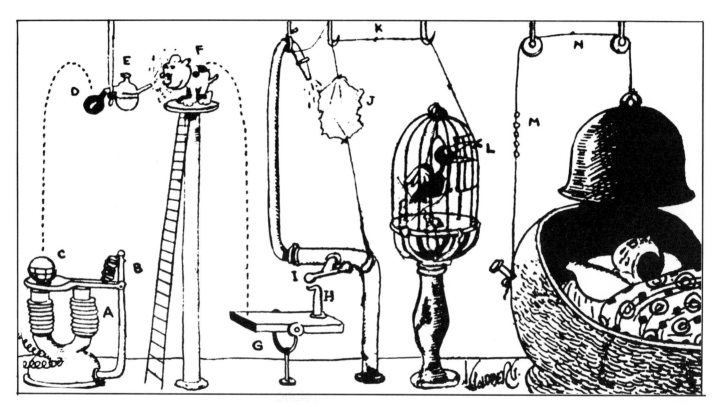

When baby cries, the vibration from voice releases electromagnet (**A**) and spring (**B**) throws iron ball (**C**) into air–Ball hits bulb (**D**) of atomizer (**E**) which contains gin–Gin sprays dog (**F**). When dog is drunk he falls over on platform (**G**), pushing point (**H**) upward and turning on faucet (**I**).

Water wets piece of old shirt (**J**) which shrinks and pulls string (**K**) opening door of cage (**L**). Bird flies out, eating bird-seed (**M**) and biting string (**N**) in two. Sound-proof bell falls down over baby's head, allowing you to remain undisturbed.

Labor-Saving Potato Masher

Cheese (**A**) gets restless and moves down incline (**B**). Duck (**C**) is overcome and falls over on platform (**D**), tossing up spiked-ball (**E**) which punctures balloon (**F**)–Policeman (**G**) hears report and thinks somebody is shot and pokes his head in the window, hitting board (**H**) and tipping over pitcher (**I**)–Water (**J**) falls into hopper (**K**) and is forced out through pipe (**L**), pressing against electric button (**M**), causing motor (**N**) to start music box (**P**), through pulley (**O**)–Shimmy Bird (**Q**) starts dancing and platform (**R**) vibrates, giving proper motion to potato masher underneath–The whole operation is repeated for each potato.

Back Scratcher

Flame from lamp (**A**) catches on curtain (**B**) and fire department sends stream of water (**C**) through window—dwarf (**D**) thinks it is raining and reaches for umbrella (**E**), pulling string (**F**) and lifting end of platform (**G**)—iron ball (**H**) falls and pulls string (**I**), causing hammer (**J**) to hit plate of glass (**K**)—crash of glass wakes up pup (**L**) and mother dog (**M**) rocks him to sleep in cradle (**N**), causing attached wooden hand (**O**) to move up and down along your back.

Simple Way to Open an Egg

When you pick up morning paper (**A**), string (**B**) opens door of birdcage (**C**) and bird (**D**) follows bird-seed (**E**) up platform (**F**) and falls over edge into pitcher of water (**G**)—water splashes on flower (**H**), which grows, pushing up rod (**I**), causing string (**J**) to fire pistol (**K**)—shot scares monkey (**L**) who jumps up, hitting head against bumper (**M**), forcing razor (**N**) down into egg (**O**). Loosened shell falls into saucer (**P**).

Keep Baby Covered at Night

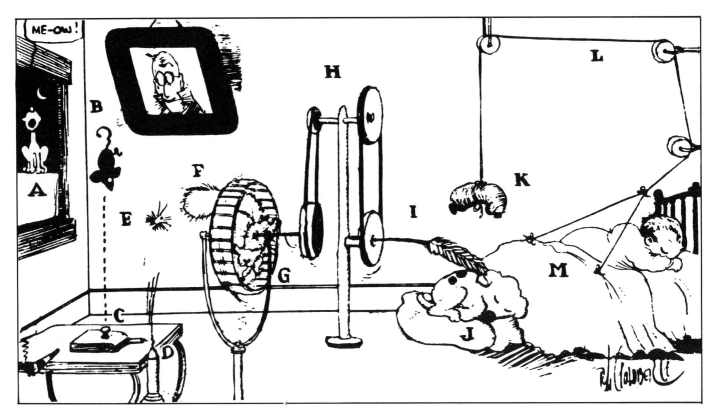

Cat on fence (**A**) scares out mouse (**B**) from behind Grandpa's picture–mouse lands on button of cigar lighter (**C**) lighting roman candle (**D**) which shoots star (**E**) scorching tail (**F**) of squirrel (**G**). Squirrel revolves in cage, setting series of belts (**H**) in motion and revolving feather (**I**) which tickles dog (**J**). Dog wakes up and grabs iron frankfurter (**K**), pulling string (**L**) which lifts cover (**M**) back on child–disappointed dog goes back to sleep and operation is repeated each time child kicks off covers.

If the Soap Falls Out of the Bathtub, Try This

Man in bathtub snaps fingers and pet Golf-Beaked Soap Hawk (**A**) hits soap (**B**) into baseball glove (**C**)–Rebound of spring (**D**) causes glove to throw soap past cat (**E**) into trough (**F**)–Breeze from flying soap causes cat to catch cold–She sneezes, blowing soap off trough–Soap hits string (**G**), which pulls trigger of pistol (**H**), shooting ram (**I**) against small car (**J**), into which soap has meantime fallen–Car carries soap up platform (**K**), dumping it back into tub and man can continue with his bath.

Patent Fan

Take hold of handles (**A**) of wheelbarrow (**B**) and start walking. Pulley (**C**) turns kicking arrangement (**D**) which annoys bear (**E**) bear suspects doll (**F**) and eats it, pulling string (**G**) which starts mechanical bird (**H**) saying, "Do you love me?" Love-bird (**I**) keeps shaking head "yes," causing fan (**J**) to move back and forth making nice breeze blow right in your face.

Clothes Brush

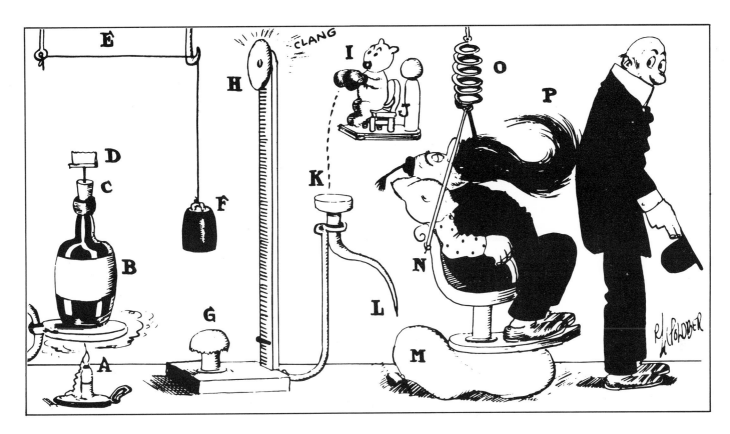

Heat from flame (**A**) expands home brew in bottle (**B**) and cork (**C**) flies out with attached safety razor blade (**D**), which cuts string (**E**)–weight (**F**) drops on strength-testing machine (**G**) ringing bell (**H**)–boxing dog (**I**) thinks round is starting and jumps off chair (**J**) falling on head of spike (**K**)–point (**L**) punctures balloon (**M**), dropping chair (**N**), which bobs up and down on spring (**O**), causing whiskers (**P**) to brush off clothes with neatness and care.

How to Cut Your Own Hair

Laughing hyena (**A**) laughs–Blind mouse (**B**) thinks hyena is laughing at him, gets insulted, walks off and bumps into disc (**C**)–Motion of disc is transferred through series of rods and discs (**D-E**) to stuffed glove (**F**), which pushes weak, starving Lilliputian Goat (**G**) against head (**H**)–Goat moves forward and eats off hair until he falls over into goat cradle (**I**) on other side when he is full.

N.B. One ordinary head of hair is just enough to fill a regulation Lilliputian Goat.

How to Scrub Your Back When You Take a Bath

Rain (**A**) goes through hose (**B**) and waters small palm (**C**)–Palm grows and tickles dog (**D**), causing him to laugh and get dignified old owl (**E**) very sore–Owl throws rock (**F**) at dog, misses him and breaks string (**G**), releasing spring (**H**) and causing ping pong racket (**I**) to swat acrobatic manikin (**J**) to swing around many times and rotate brush (**K**). At times, this device might prove slightly inconvenient because you have to wait for rain.

Fish an Olive Out of a Long-Necked Bottle

At 6:30 weight (**A**) automatically drops on head of dwarf (**B**), causing him to yell and drop cigar (**C**), which sets fire to paper (**D**)—heat from fire angers dwarf's wife (**E**)—she sharpens potato knife (**F**) on grindstone (**G**) which turns wheel (**H**) causing olive spoon (**I**) to dip repeatedly into olives—if spoon does not lift an olive in 15 minutes, clock (**J**) automatically pushes glass-cutter (**K**) against bottle and takes a chunk of glass big enough for you to stick your finger in and pull out an olive.

Life-Saving Bathing Device

Hat (**A**) has glass bowl top (**B**) containing fish (**C**)—When you sink, rubber ball (**D**) floats on surface, uncovering hole on top of bowl—Fish swims out, causing string (**E**) to set off depth-bomb (**F**)—Explosion blows iron banana (**G**) off small boat tied to swimmer's big toe (**H**)—Sinking banana pulls down strong arm (**I**) and hand (**J**) takes good grip on bathing suit—Hungry shark eats banana, relieving weight on arm and spring (**K**) causes hand to jerk you out of water to safety.

Mosquito Bite Scratcher

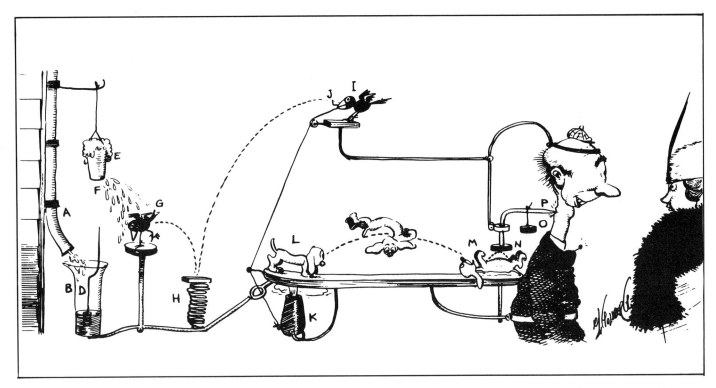

Water from drain-pipe (**A**) drops into flask (**B**)–cork (**C**) rises with water carrying needle (**D**) with it–needle punctures paper tumbler (**E**) containing beer (**F**)–beer sprinkles over bluebird (**G**) and he becomes intoxicated and falls on spring (**H**), which bounces him to platform (**I**)–he pulls string (**J**) thinking it is a worm–string fires off cannon (**K**) which frightens peace-hound (**L**), causing him to jump in air, landing on back in position (**M**)–his heavy breathing raises disc (**N**), which is brought back into its original position by weight (**O**),–the continual breathing of the dog moves scratcher (**P**) up and down over mosquito bite, causing no embarrassment while talking to a lady.

Self-Working Corkscrew

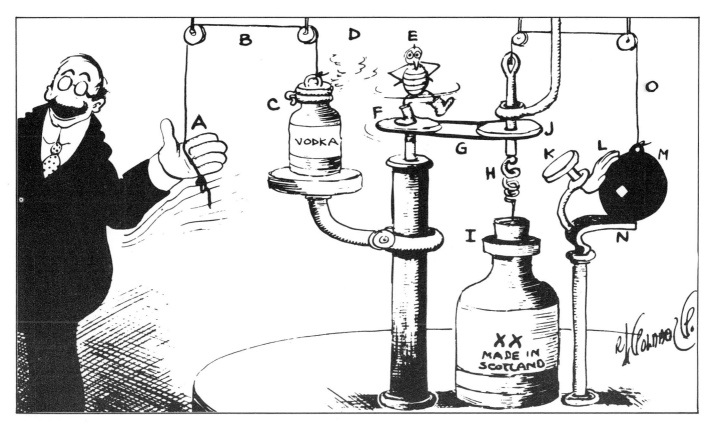

When you say "have a drink," natural motion of hand (**A**) pulls string (**B**) and lifts lid (**C**), releasing vodka fumes (**D**) which make Russian dancing bug (**E**) feel giddy–he starts dancing national dance of Russia and revolves platform (**F**)–pulley (**G**) turns corkscrew (**H**) and it sinks into cork (**I**) bringing down disc (**J**), which hits surface (**K**) and causes wooden hand (**L**) to push iron ball (**M**) off support (**N**), causing cord (**O**) to pull corkscrew with cork from bottle.

How to Tie a Bow Tie

Place crumb (**A**) on window sill and wait for sparrow (**B**) to enter–Let go of string (**C**)–Weight (**D**) falls on sparrow, knocking him into pail of water (**E**)–Water (**F**) splashes on sponge (**G**), causing it to get heavier and start spring (**H**) vibrating–Saw (**I**), attached to spring, saws off end of log (**J**), which falls on string (**K**), ringing gong (**L**), causing worms (**M**) wearing boxing gloves, to get mixed up in a scrap–as they twist and squirm, they should work bow tie into some sort of a knot–If this knot doesn't look good, reach up and grab ready-made slip-under-collar tie (**N**) and everthing is jake.

Simple Cigar Lighter

Go to ball grounds and stand near fence (**A**)–during game, ball (**B**) is knocked over fence and hits dog (**C**) pushing him to ground–string (**D**), tied to dog's tail pulls cork (**E**) from champagne bottle (**F**)–sound of wine being opened causes waiter (**G**) to expect big tip and he extends right hand in receptive position–it starts to rain–rain falls in waiter's hand and runs in steady stream into pipe (**H**)–water finally drops on blade of grass (**I**)–grass grows until it tickles soft-shell crab (**J**) under the chin, making him laugh–he falls to platform (**L**), moving spring (**M**) downward and pulling string (**N**) which opens box (**O**) and releases firefly (**P**)–firefly, thinking picture of candle (**Q**) is real thing, gets jealous and springs upon it, passing cigar (**R**), and giving it required light.

Bottle Opener

Elephant (**A**) eats peanuts (**B**)–as bag gets lighter weight (**C**) drops and spike (**D**) punctures balloon (**E**)–explosion scares monkey (**F**)–his hat (**G**) flies off and releases hook (**H**), causing spring (**I**) to pull string (**J**) which tilts tennis racket (**K**)– racket hits ball (**L**), making it spin around on attached string, thereby screwing corkscrew into cork (**M**)–ball hits sleeping dog (**N**) who jumps and pulls cork out of bottle with string (**O**)–my how simple!

Self-Shining Shoes

Professor Lucifer Gorgonzola Butts A.K. invents simple self-shining shoes–as passerby steps rudely on your shoes, you bend over, causing string (**A**) to pull open accordion (**B**), sounding note (**C**)–dancing mouse (**D**) starts waltzing and steps on trigger of pistol (**E**)–bullet (**F**) disengages hook (**G**) and allows arrow (**H**) to shoot out, pulling cord (**I**) which opens inverted box (**J**), dropping bone (**K**)–pet dog (**L**) sees bone, wags tail, causing brush (**M**) to spread polish (**N**) which drops from hole in derby (**O**).

Easy Way to Open a Window

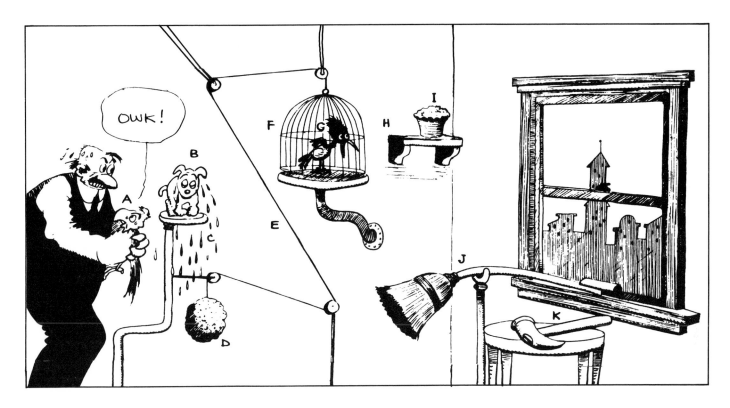

After trying unsuccessfully to open window for half an hour, you relieve your anger by choking parrot (**A**)–dog (**B**) hears parrot's groans and weeps out of sympathy–tears (**C**) soak sponge (**D**), causing its weight to pull string (**E**) which lifts top off cage (**F**) and releases woodpecker (**G**)– woodpecker chews away shelf (**H**) and heavy biscuit (**I**) falls on broom-handle (**J**), causing it to act as lever in raising window–after repeating this operation six times without success, take hammer (**K**) and break glass in window, allowing fresh air to enter room.

Fire Extinguisher

Professor Butts, training for the Olympic Games, broad jumps into the Grand Canyon by mistake and, before he reaches bottom, has plenty of time to invent a neat little fire extinguisher.

Porter (**A**) smells smoke coming from room and in the excitement sticks his head through window screen to investigate. Little boy, remembering carnival, throws baseball (**B**) which bounces off porter's head and breaks glass in aquarium (**C**), causing water to run into trough (**D**) and revolve paddle wheel (**E**), which winds rope (**F**), pulling knife (**G**) and cutting cord (**H**). Shoe (**I**) falls on baby's face, baby sheds copious tears. Splashing of tears makes bullfrog (**J**) think of babbling brook and he starts swimming, causing file (**K**) to cut chain (**L**) which breaks and allows trees (**M**) to snap upright and pull wet blanket (**N**) over burning waste basket, thereby extinguishing fire.

If the fire doesn't happen to be in the waste basket, call out the fire department.

Locate Lost Golf Balls

Professor Butts puts his head in a nutcracker and squeezes out an idea to locate lost golf balls.

Hang golf bag (**A**) on hook (**B**) which pulls cord (**C**) and tilts paddle (**D**), tossing basketball (**E**) into basket (**F**). Weight of ball releases hook (**G**) and allows spring (**H**) to push head-guard (**I**) into stomach of toy clown (**J**) who claps cymbals (**K**) on rubber bulb (**L**), squirting stream of water (**M**) which starts phonograph (**N**) playing "Sonny Boy." Song awakens mother love in Snozzle Bird (**O**). She longs for a son and looks around for an egg to hatch until she finds golf ball (**P**) which she naturally mistakes for the coveted egg.

If the Snozzle Bird wants a daughter, have the phonograph play "Ramona."

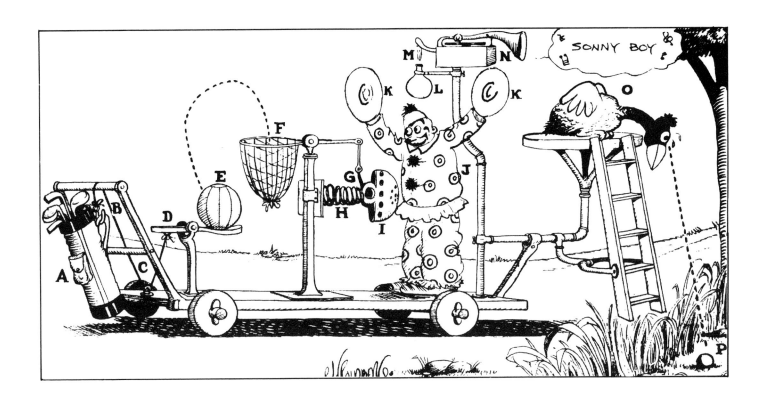

Simplified Egg Shampoo

Professor Butts sweeps the dust out of his brain and uncovers an idea for a simplified egg shampoo.

Neglect to pay your butcher bill and when butcher comes around for money he opens door (**A**) which pulls cord (**B**), releasing Jack-in-the-Box (**C**) which presses head against button (**D**), turning on flashlight (**E**). Hen (**F**) thinks sun has risen and lays egg (**G**) which rolls down trough (**H**) and breaks against your head (**I**). Sudden impact of egg causes you to duck and pull string (**J**) which tilts sanitary soap-container (**K**), causing soap to splash on head. You reach for something with which to steady yourself and grab weight (**L**) that starts cuckoo clock (**M**), causing pendulum (**N**) to rub attached brush (**O**) back and forth on hair.

On second thought, it may be advisable to go to the barber shop for your egg shampoo because if the clock gets out of order it will cost much more to hire a watchmaker.

Awning That Lowers Itself

Professor Butts chokes on a fish bone and coughs up an idea for an awning that lowers itself when the sun comes out.

Sunlight (**A**) shining through magnifying glass (**B**) burns rope (**C**) which separates and allows bent tree (**D**) to snap back and catapult harpoon (**E**) into neck of pet whale (**F**). Pain in the neck causes him to spout with anguish, thereby sprinkling plant (**G**). As plant grows it lifts end of see-saw (**H**) and pushes spike (**I**) into balloon (**J**), causing it to burst with loud report. Professional orator (**K**) thinks it is a firecracker and stands up to make a Fourth of July speech. Hot air lights candle (**L**) which burns rope (**M**), allowing awning (**N**) to drop.

If awning catches fire and the house burns down, it will let in even more sunlight.

Painless Tooth Extractor

Professor Butts evolves his latest painless tooth extractor in a state of scientific delirium.

Dentist (**A**) rushes out of door (**B**) into stockbroker's office next door to see what Consolidated Boloney is doing. In his haste he loses rubber heel (**C**) which bounces into cup (**D**), tipping lever (**E**) which pulls string (**F**), upsetting bag of peanuts (**G**). Squirrel (**H**) revolves cage (**I**) in mad attempt to grab peanuts and causes piston (**J**) to work bellows (**K**)—motion of bellows lifts cover (**L**) and at the same time blows fumes of Limburger cheese (**M**) in face of patient, knocking him cold. Vibrations of his head while snoring cause string (**N**) to pull delicate prop (**O**) from under shelf (**P**) and sudden drop of weight (**Q**) results in wire (**R**) pulling tooth. Falling weight also causes paddle (**S**) to toss glass of water (**T**) in patient's face to revive him.

If he has not revived when the dentist comes back three days later, the grand jury will have to decide who is to be tried for murder, the dentist or the man who sold him the limburger cheese.

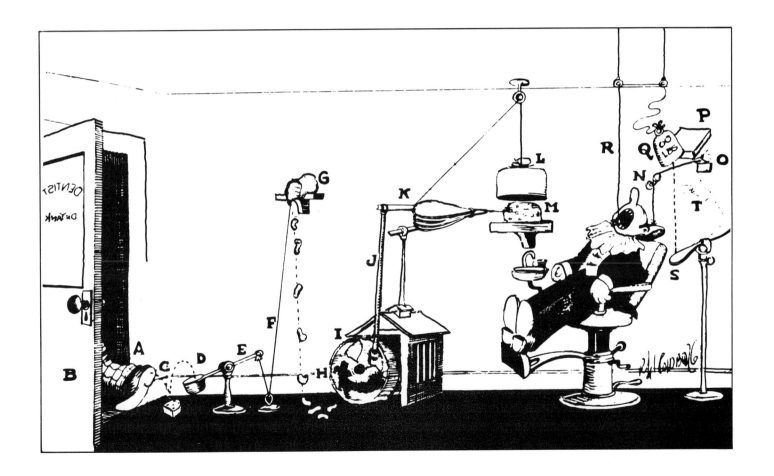

Fly Swatter

A safe falls on the head of Professor Butts and knocks out an idea for his latest simple fly swatter.

Carbolic acid (**A**) drips on string (**B**), causing it to break and release elastic of bean shooter (**C**) which projects ball (**D**) into bunch of garlic (**E**), causing it to fall into syrup can (**F**) and splash syrup violently against side wall. Fly (**G**) buzzes with glee and goes for syrup, his favorite dish. Butler dog (**H**) mistakes hum of fly's wings for door buzzer and runs to meet visitor, pulling rope (**I**) which turns stop-go signal (**J**) and causes baseball (**K**) to sock fly who falls to floor unconscious.

As fly drops to floor pet trout (**L**) jumps for him, misses, and lands in net (**M**). Weight of fish forces shoe (**N**) down on fallen fly and puts him out of the running for all time.

If the fish catches the fly, the shoe can be used for cracking nuts.

How to Keep Shop Windows Clean

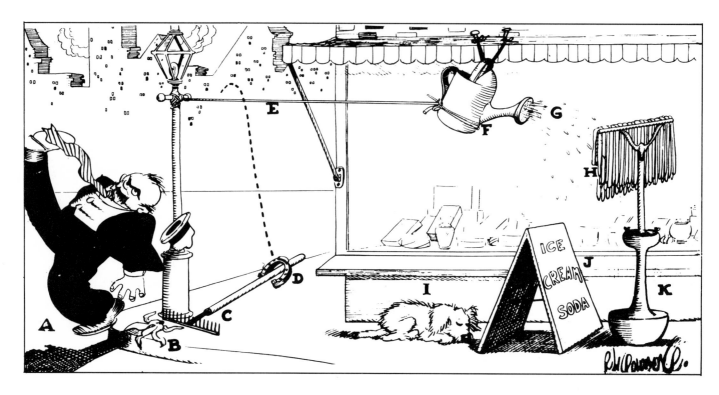

Professor Butts stands in front of an x-ray and sees an idea inside his head showing how to keep shop windows clean.

Passing man (**A**) slips on banana peel (**B**) causing him to fall on rake (**C**)–as handle of rake rises it throws horseshoe (**D**) onto rope (**E**) which sags, thereby tilting sprinkling can (**F**). Water (**G**) saturates mop (**H**), Pickle Terrier (**I**) thinks it is raining, gets up to run into house and upsets sign, (**J**) throwing it against non-tipping cigar ash receiver (**K**) which causes it to swing back and forth and swish the mop against window pane, wiping it clean.

If man breaks his neck by fall, move away before cop arrives.

Self-Working Tire Pump

Professor Butts brushes his hair and an idea for a self-working tire pump is found among the dandruff.

Mechanic (**A**) goes to get gasoline and turns pump handle (**B**) which works piston rod (**C**) and raises jack (**D**). Jack, pushing against bar (**E**), causes it to pull rope (**F**) and raise awning (**G**), exposing sign (**H**). Scotchman (**I**), seeing sign announcing the distribution of free lunch, plays fast tune on bagpipe (**J**) in a joyous delirium and escaping air goes into attached hose (**K**) inflating tire (**L**).

Of course, you don't have to serve free lunch because, by the time the Scotchman finds it out, the automobile will be well on its way.

Self-Rolling Rug

Professor Butts flies through the windshield of his car and when they pick out the broken glass they find an idea for a self-rolling rug.

Place fresh pie (**A**) on window sill (**B**) to cool. When tramp (**C**) sneaks up to steal it, housemaid (**D**) falls back with fright into rocking chair (**E**) which tilts pedestal (**F**), causing marble statue of diving Venus (**G**) to dive into goldfish bowl (**H**) and splash water on plant (**I**) which grows and turns on switch (**J**) of radio (**K**) which plays old tune called "Oceana Roll." Little trick rolling circus elephant (**L**), hearing tune, does his stuff and keeps rolling over and over until rug (**M**) is completely wrapped around him and floor is cleared for dancing.

Rug wrapped around delicate little elephant also keeps him from catching cold from draft coming through open window.

Slicing Bread for the Picnic Sandwich

Professor Butts trips over a rug and, while looking at the stars, discovers an idea for slicing bread for the picnic sandwich.

Rising sun (**A**) ripens peaches (**B**) which fall on beehive (**C**), scaring out bees (**D**) which sting sleeping individual (**E**). Sudden pain causes him to double up and kick legs. Spear (**F**) punctures inner tube (**G**). Pressure of escaping air pushes cannon ball (**H**) off shelf (**I**), knocking over scarecrow (**J**), which clutches farmer (**K**) from the rear. Farmer, believing he is being attacked by a bandit, starts driving home like mad causing discs (**L**) on disc-harrow to slice bread (**M**) in even pieces.

This invention isn't really very important because somebody usually gets bitten by a snake early in the day and the picnic busts up before you get a chance to eat any lunch.

Can Opener

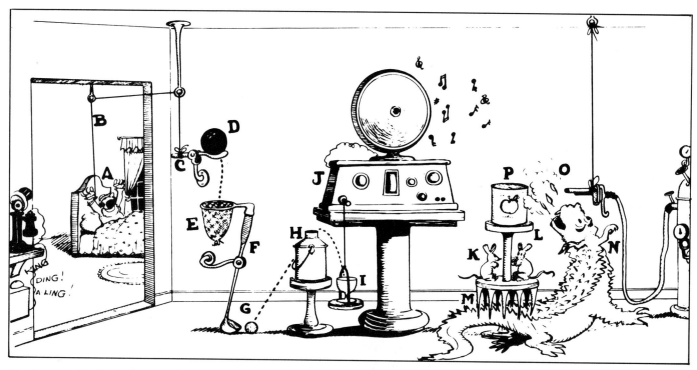

Professor Butts falls on his head and dopes out a simple can opener while he is still groggy. Go outside and call up your home. When phone bell rings, maid (**A**) mistakes it for an alarm clock–she awakens and stretches, pulling cord (**B**) which raises end of ladle (**C**). Ball (**D**) drops into net (**E**), causing golf club (**F**) to swing against ball (**G**), making a clean drive and upsetting milk can (**H**). Milk spills into glass (**I**) and the weight pulls switch on radio (**J**). Waltzing mice (**K**) hear music and proceed to dance, causing revolving apparatus (**L**) to spin and turn. Spikes (**M**) scratch tail of pet dragon (**N**) who in anger emits fire, igniting acetylene torch (**O**) and burning off top of tomato can (**P**) as it rotates.

When not opening cans, the dragon can always be kept busy chasing away income tax investigators and prohibition officers.

Pencil Sharpener

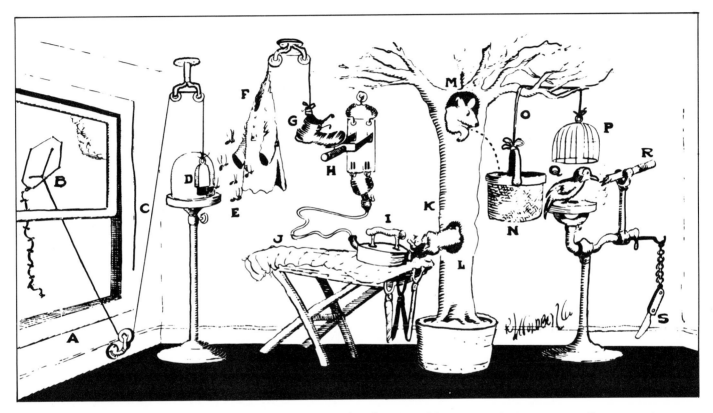

Professor Butts gets his think-tank working and evolves the simplified pencil sharpener.

Open window (**A**) and fly kite (**B**). String (**C**) lifts small door (**D**), allowing moths (**E**) to escape and eat red flannel shirt (**F**). As weight of shirt becomes less, shoe (**G**) steps on switch (**H**) which heats electric iron (**I**) and burns hole in pants (**J**). Smoke (**K**) enters hole in tree (**L**), smoking out opossum (**M**) which jumps into basket (**N**), pulling rope (**O**) and lifting cage (**P**), allowing woodpecker (**Q**) to chew wood from pencil (**R**), exposing lead. Emergency knife (**S**) is always handy in case opossum or the woodpecker gets sick and can't work.

Self-Watering Palm Tree

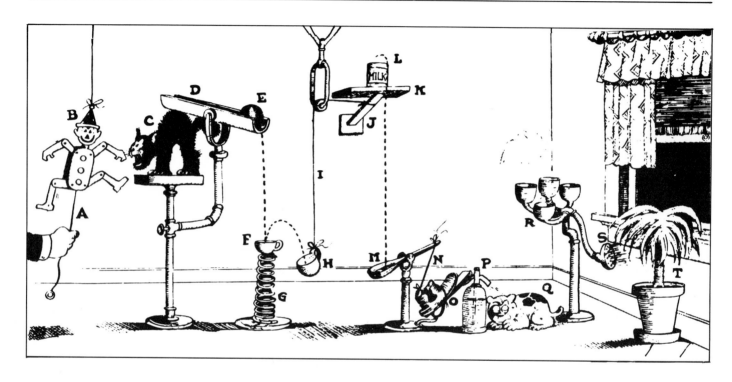

Professor Butt's brain takes a nose dive and out comes his self-watering palm tree.

String (**A**) works jumping jack (**B**), frightening cat (**C**) which raises back and lifts trough (**D**), causing ball (**E**) to fall into teacup (**F**). Spring (**G**) makes ball rebound into cup (**H**), pulling on string (**I**) which releases stick (**J**), causing shelf (**K**) to collapse. Milk can (**L**) drops on ladle (**M**) and tension on string (**N**) tilts shoe (**O**) against jigger on seltzer bottle (**P**), squirting seltzer on ash-can spaniel (**Q**) who hasn't had a bath in four years. Surprise causes him to turn three somersaults over apparatus (**R**) and water splashes naturally into bowls, running through spray (**S**), watering palm (**T**), and saving yourself a trip to Havana for tropical atmosphere.

Self-Sharpening Razor Blade

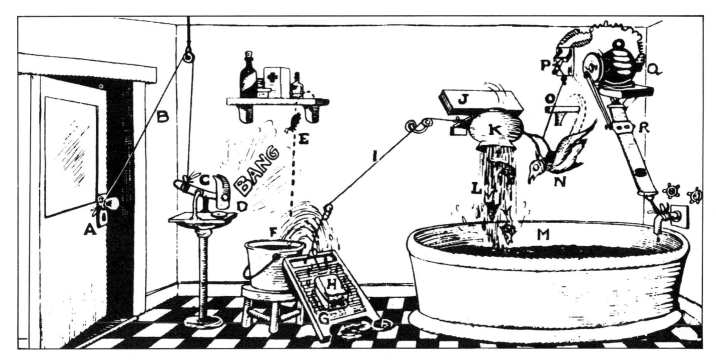

The professor takes a swig of Goofy Oil and invents the self-sharpening razor blade.

Wind blows open door (**A**), pulling string (**B**) which causes hammer (**C**) to explode cap (**D**). Peaceful cockroach (**E**) loses balance from fright and falls into pail of water (**F**). Water splashes on washboard (**G**), soap (**H**) slides over surface, pulling string (**I**), yanking out prop from under shelf (**J**) and upsetting bowl (**K**). Goldfish (**L**) fall into bath tub (**M**) and hungry seagull (**N**) swoops down on them, thereby pulling string (**O**) which turns on switch (**P**), starting motor (**Q**) and causing razor blade (**R**) to move up and down along strap (**S**).

It is advisable to live near a barber shop in case there is no wind to blow the door open in the first place.

Digging Up Bait for Fishing

A barber puts a scalding towel on Professor Butts's face and while he is screaming with pain he thinks up an invention for digging up bait for fishing. The maid (**A**) peels an onion and cries into funnel (**B**). Tears (**C**) run through pipe (**D**) and drip into pan (**E**) of jeweler's scale (**F**), causing end of bar (**G**) to press against small bellows (**H**) which blow insect powder (**I**) on shelf and knock off roaches (**J**). Roaches fall on edge of antique fan (**K**), causing it to close and expose surface of mirror (**L**). Selfish Palooka Hound (**M**) sees his reflection in mirror and, thinking it is another dog, hastens to bury bone (**N**). As he digs, he uncovers worm (**O**) which is seen immediately by early bird (**P**) who dives for it off perch. Weight (**Q**) drops on head of bird and knocks him cold just as he pulls worm far enough out of ground for fisherman to grab it easily.

When the early bird wakes up you can let him eat the onion just so he will not be getting too raw a deal.

Anti-Floor Walking Device

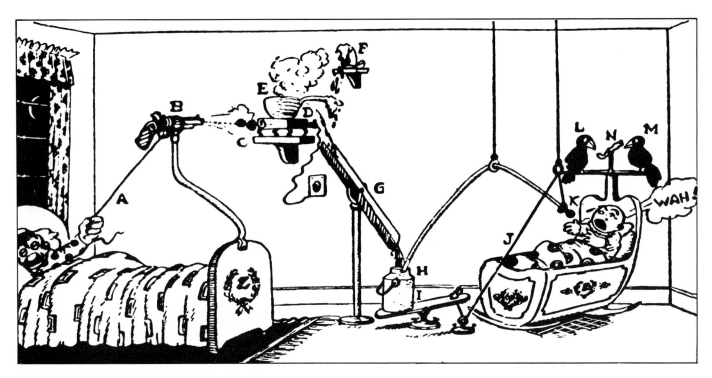

The professor's brain tosses off his latest anti-floor walking paraphernalia.

Pull string (**A**) which discharges pistol (**B**) and bullet (**C**) hits switch on electric stove (**D**), warming pot of milk (**E**). Vapor from milk melts candle (**F**) which drips on handle of pot, causing it to upset and spill milk down trough (**G**) and into can (**H**)–weight bears down on lever (**I**), pulling string (**J**) which brings nursing nipple (**K**) within baby's reach.

In the meantime baby's yelling has awakened two pet crows (**L&M**) and they discover rubber worm (**N**) which they proceed to eat. Unable to masticate it, they pull it back and forth causing cradle to rock and put baby to sleep.

Put cotton in your ears so you will not be bothered if baby wakes again.

Machine for Washing Dishes

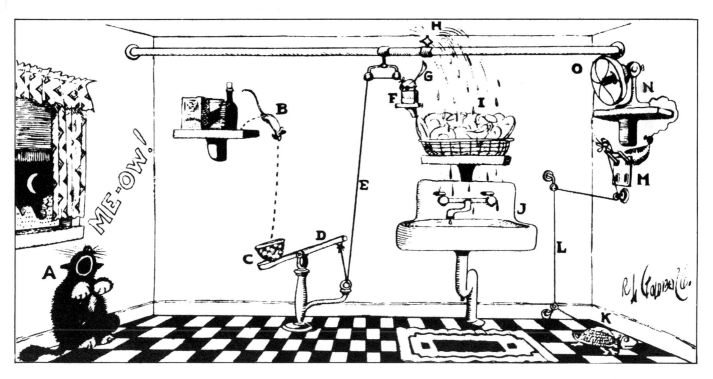

The professor turns on his think-faucet and dopes out a machine for washing dishes while you are at the movies.

When spoiled tomcat (**A**) discovers he is alone, he lets out a yell which scares mouse (**B**) into jumping into basket (**C**), causing lever end (**D**) to rise and pull string (**E**) which snaps automatic cigar-lighter (**F**). Flame (**G**) starts fire sprinkler (**H**). Water runs on dishes (**I**) and drips into sink (**J**). Turtle (**K**), thinking he hears babbling brook babbling, and having no sense of direction, starts wrong way and pulls string (**L**), which turns on switch (**M**) that starts electric glow heater (**N**). Heat ray (**O**) dries the dishes.

If the cat and the turtle get on to your scheme and refuse to cooperate, simply put the dishes on the front porch and pray for rain.

Closing the Window

The professor takes a pill and dopes out a device for closing the window if it starts to rain while you're away.

Pet bullfrog (**A**), homesick for water, hears rainstorm and jumps for joy, pulling string (**B**) which opens catch (**C**) and releases hot water bag (**D**), allowing it to slide under chair (**E**). Heat raises yeast (**F**), lifting disk (**G**) which causes hook (**H**) to release spring (**I**). Toy automobile bumper (**J**) socks monkey (**K**) in the neck, putting him down for the count on table (**L**). He staggers to his feet and slips on banana peel (**M**). He instinctively reaches for flying rings (**N**) to avoid further disaster and his weight pulls rope (**O**), closing window (**P**), stopping the rain from leaking through on the family downstairs and thinning their soup.

Automatic Sheet Music Turner

At last! The great brain of the distinguished man of science gives the world the simple automatic sheet music turner!

Press left foot (**A**) on pedal (**B**) which pulls down handle (**C**) on tire pump (**D**). Pressure of air blows whistle (**E**)–goldfish (**F**) believes this is dinner signal and starts feeding on worm (**G**). The pull on string (**H**) releases brace (**I**), dropping shelf (**J**), leaving weight (**K**) without support. Naturally, hatrack (**L**) is suddenly extended and boxing glove (**M**) hits punching bag (**N**) which, in turn, is punctured by spike (**O**).

Escaping air blows against sail (**P**) which is attached to page of music (**Q**), which turns gently and makes way for the next outburst of sweet or sour melody.

Putting Postage Stamps on Envelopes

The massive intellect of Professor Butts evolves a simple appliance for putting postage stamps on envelopes.

Boss (**A**) sneezes, Snozzlehound (**B**), frightened out of a sound slumber, runs out of the office, upsetting hatrack (**C**) and breaking the ice-water container (**D**). Water (**E**) is spilled into trough (**F**) and is then conveyed to bucket (**G**).

The weight of the water in bucket causes string (**H**) to compress nutcracker (**I**) which squeezes bulb on medicine-dropper (**J**) and moistens postage stamp (**K**).

Stenographer (**L**), about to go out to lunch, hears the splashing of water on several occasions during the operation of the apparatus. She thinks it is raining and picks up her umbrella (**M**), which pulls back small hook (**N**), causing spring (**P**) to throw paddle (**O**) over on envelope (**Q**) and press moistened stamp in place.

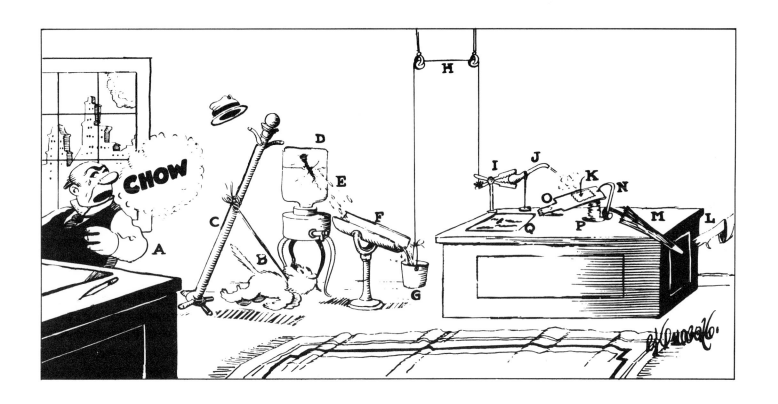

Typewriter Eraser

Professor Butts chokes on a prune pit and coughs up an idea for an automatic typewriter eraser. Ring for office boy (**A**), who comes running in and stumbles over feet of window cleaner (**B**). He grabs for hat-rack (**C**) to save himself. Hat-rack falls against books (**D**) which drop on ruler (**E**), causing pen (**F**) to fly up and puncture balloon (**G**) which explodes with a loud report.

Trained monkey (**H**) mistakes report for gun that is the signal to begin his vaudeville act and he starts pedalling like mad. The rubber tire (**I**) passes over paper (**J**) and erases mistake made by sleepy stenographer who is too tired to do it herself because she had such a long walk home from an automobile ride the night before.

It is advisable to have your office over a garage so you can get quick service in case of a puncture.

Idea for Dodging Bill Collectors

Professor Butts mistakes a lot of broken glass for bath salts and when they pull him out of the tub he mumbles an idea for dodging bill collectors.

As tailor (**A**) fits customer (**B**) and calls out measurements, college boy (**C**) mistakes them for football signals and makes a flying tackle at clothing dummy (**D**). Dummy bumps head against paddle (**E**), causing it to pull hook (**F**) and throw bottle (**G**) on end of folding hatrack (**H**) which spreads and pushes head of cabbage (**I**) into net (**J**). Weight of cabbage pulls cord (**K**), causing shears (**L**) to cut string (**M**). Bag of sand (**N**) drops on scale (**O**) and pushes broom (**P**) against pail of whitewash (**Q**) which upsets all over you causing you to look like a marble statue and making it impossible for you to be recognized by bill collectors.

Don't worry about posing as any particular historical statue because bill collectors don't know much about art.

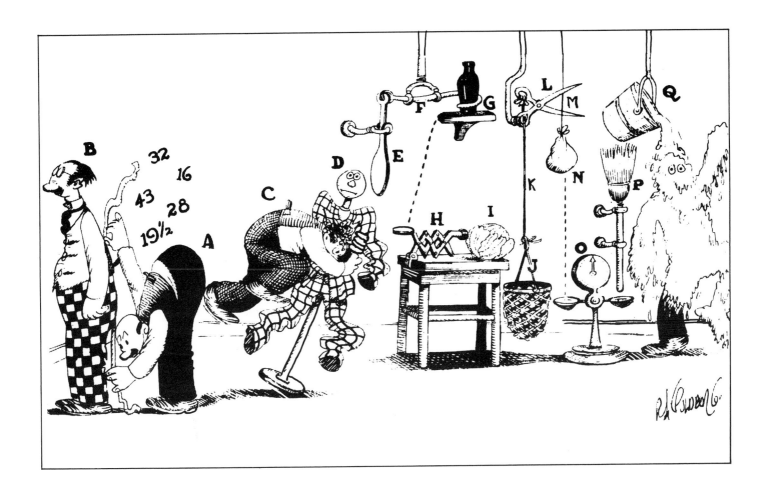

Wholesale Mosquito Destroyer

Professor Butts goes to a chiropractor and, while doubled up in a knot, thinks of a patent wholesale mosquito-destroyer. Owl (**A**) flies away into the night, causing branch (**B**) to vibrate and pull cord (**C**), rubbing match (**D**) against brick (**E**). As match lights from friction it ignites fuse (**F**) which lights lamp in magic lantern (**G**) and throws picture of bald-headed man (**H**) on floor of porch. Hungry mosquitoes seeing bald head gather for a banquet and buzz so loudly that hired girl (**I**) thinks somebody is sawing wood. She runs in with dustpan to sweep up sawdust and steps on loose board (**J**) which causes string (**K**) to upset bottle of acid (**L**). Acid eats into rope (**M**) causing it to break. Heavy occupant of hammock crashes on mosquitoes killing them wholesale.

Of course, this will not do for daylight mosquito-killing as the owl will not fly away until evening. A few mosquito bites during the day won't do any harm because you can get plenty of exercise scratching them.

61

Idea for Whipping Cream

Professor Butts, while looking for a bothersome moth in his whiskers, finds a great idea for whipping cream. As you take broom (**A**) and sweep down cobweb (**B**), spider (**C**) falls on electric switch (**D**) and turns on motor (**E**) which revolves clothes wringer (**F**), thereby winding rope (**G**) and pulling suit of armor (**H**) down stairs–hearing tinny noise master (**I**) thinks someone is stealing his flivver. He jumps up and opens window (**J**) which pulls string (**K**) and closes shears (**L**), clipping off frankfurter (**M**) which falls in front of bologna hound (**N**). Dog grabs it and runs away with it, pulling fishing line (**O**) which causes reel handle (**P**) to rotate rapidly and whip the cream.

If you don't like shortcake, you can use the whipped cream for shaving.

Keep You From Forgetting to Mail Your Wife's Letter

Professor Butts gets caught in a revolving door and becomes dizzy enough to dope out an idea to keep you from forgetting to mail your wife's letter.

As you walk past cobbler shop, hook (**A**) strikes suspended boot (**B**), causing it to kick football (**C**) through goal posts (**D**). Football drops into basket (**E**) and string (**F**) tilts sprinkling can, (**G**) causing water to soak coat tails (**H**). As coat shrinks cord (**I**) opens door (**J**) of cage, allowing bird (**K**) to walk out on perch (**L**) and grab worm (**M**) which is attached to string (**N**). This pulls down window shade (**O**) on which is written, "YOU SAP, MAIL THAT LETTER." A simple way to avoid all this trouble is to marry a wife who can't write.

Dusting Off Radio

Professor Butts dives into an empty swimming pool and finds a simple idea for dusting off the radio.

As acid (**A**) drops into water (**B**) it causes hydrometer (**C**) to rise and push against swinging shelf (**D**), causing candle (**E**) to fall into grate (**F**) and set fire to logs. Heat from burning logs hatches cocoons (**G**)—as happy butterflies (**H**) emerge they flap their wings violently and breeze blows against sail (**I**) which swings around and causes hunting knife (**J**) to cut cord (**K**). Flat iron (**L**) drops and pulls away clamp (**M**), releasing spring (**N**) which vibrates and causes grain of corn (**O**) to bob up and down–Zopple Bird (**P**) jumps up and down in effort to grab corn and dusts off radio with tail.

If Zopple Bird succeeds in grabbing the corn before the radio is thoroughly dusted, finish the job with your uncle's whiskers.

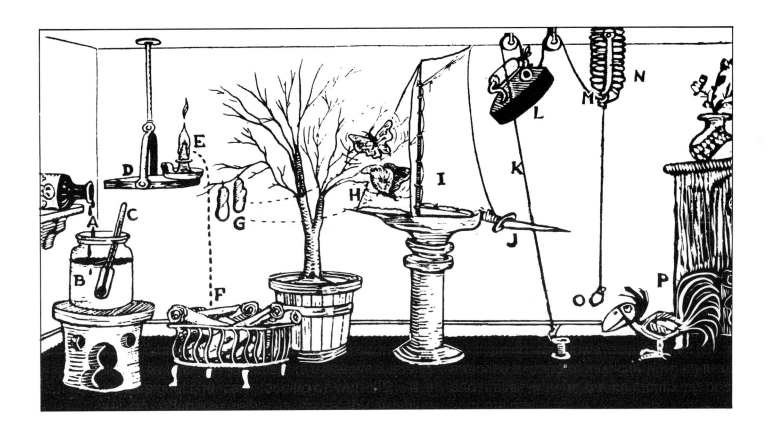

Cooling a Plate of Soup

Professor Butts, taking his morning exercise, kicks himself in the nose and sees a simple idea for cooling a plate of soup. Chef (**A**) carelessly spills dish of hot chili con carne (**B**) which scalds pet porcupine (**C**) who raises his quills in pain. Quills come through cane bottom chair (**D**) and cause proprietor (**E**) to jump and hit shelf (**F**), upsetting beer stein (**G**). As stein drops it pulls string, (**H**) causing bellows (**I**) to inflate gas bag (**J**) which swells and upsets tray (**K**), throwing dishes (**L**) to the floor with a terrific crash. Love-sick alley cat (**M**), thinking someone is throwing things at him, runs in fright on top of circular fence (**N**). He is completely exhausted when he reaches the bottom and stands puffing in front of soup (**O**) until it is cooled.

After the meal, the porcupine can spare a few quills for toothpicks.

Self-Working Fishing Line

Professor Butts steps on a third rail and works out an idea for a self-working fishing line.

As fish (**A**) bites on hook (**B**), he pulls fishing line (**C**) and causes heavy wire (**D**) to vibrate and work butcher's saw (**E**) back and forth, cutting oar (**F**) in two allowing oar to fall into water and splash. Life-saving channel hound (**G**) thinks someone has fallen overboard and dives into water, pulling string (**H**) and upsetting yeast solution on log (**I**)–as log swells it breaks cord (**J**), allowing sinker (**K**) to drop on insect gun (**L**) which blows snuff (**M**) into face of fisherman (**N**), causing him to sneeze and turn windmill (**O**) which winds line and brings in fish.

If the fisherman does not wake up for a few days, the fish may be too old to eat. But it will be dry enough to have framed and hung in the billard room.

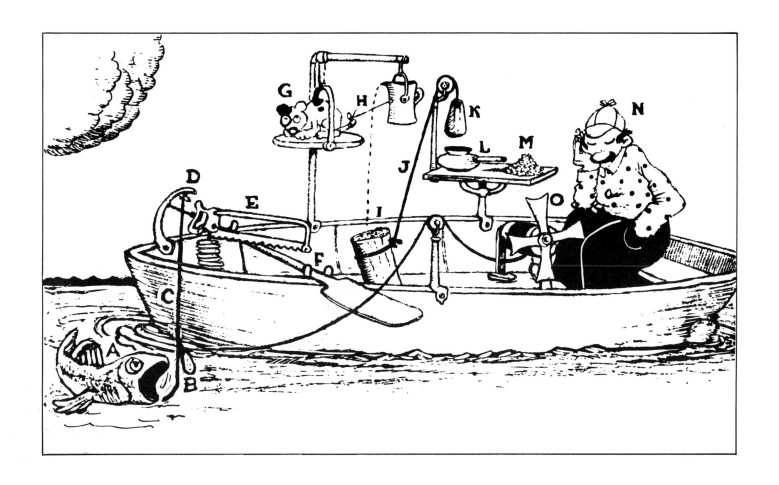

Simple Way to Sharpen Ice Skates

Professor Butts, while overhauling a 1907 Ford, finds an idea for a simple way to sharpen ice skates.

Wire bundle-basket (**A**) in sporting store hits floor walker (**B**) and knocks him dizzy. As he sinks to floor his knees hit end of see-saw (**C**) which tosses basket ball (**D**) into broken net (**E**). Ball falls on tennis racket (**F**), causing group of tin cans (**G**) to fly up out of reach of hungry goat (**H**). Goat, being robbed of his dinner, jumps in fury and butts his head against boxing dummy (**I**). Dummy sways back and forth on swivel base (**J**), causing two eccentric wheels (**K**) to push file (**L**) across blade of skate (**M**) and make it sharp enough to use for skating in the winter and shaving in the summer.

You may think it cruel to hit the floor-walker on the head. But we assure you there is nothing inside which can be damaged.

Turning on the Steam Before You Get Out of Bed

The professor puts the wrong end of his cigar in his mouth and spits out an idea for turning on the steam before you get out of bed.

Early morning sun (**A**) shines through magnifying glass (**B**) which focuses ray on foot (**C**). As foot is drawn away in pain string (**D**) causes razor (**E**) to cut cord (**F**) and release beaver (**G**). Beaver gnaws clothes tree (**H**) which he mistakes for a young sapling. Clothes (**I**) fall on paddle (**J**), causing end to pull cork (**K**) from champagne bottle (**L**) with a loud report. Passing policeman thinks he hears pistol shot, opens window (**M**) to investigate and causes string (**N**) to work lighter (**O**) which lights Fourth of July pinwheel (**P**) which revolves and turns on the radiator.

Of course the big problem is where to get the champagne. And after that you must make it a point to get out of bed before the policeman can drink it.

Simple Way to Make Your Own Toast

Professor Butts, being a poor old bachelor, is forced to dope out this simple way to make his own toast.

Wait patiently for snowstorm. As snow (**A**) falls on shovel (**B**) it causes string (**C**) to turn on electric switch (**D**) which lights sun ray lamp (**E**). Heat rays start toasting slice of bread and also cover baby (**F**) with coat of tan. Near-sighted mother (**G**), mistaking tan for dirt, throws water over baby. Water, splashing on mill-wheel (**H**), causes it to revolve and rotate forks (**I**), which keep toasted bread turning.

Wind from revolving toast blows against sail (**J**), which forces butcher's cleaver (**K**) down against string (**L**), thereby cutting string and causing boxing glove (**M**) to shoot out and force shoe (**N**) to kick toasted bread onto your plate.

Before trying this method be sure you are in a country where they have snow. Otherwise, you will wait around until you starve to death.

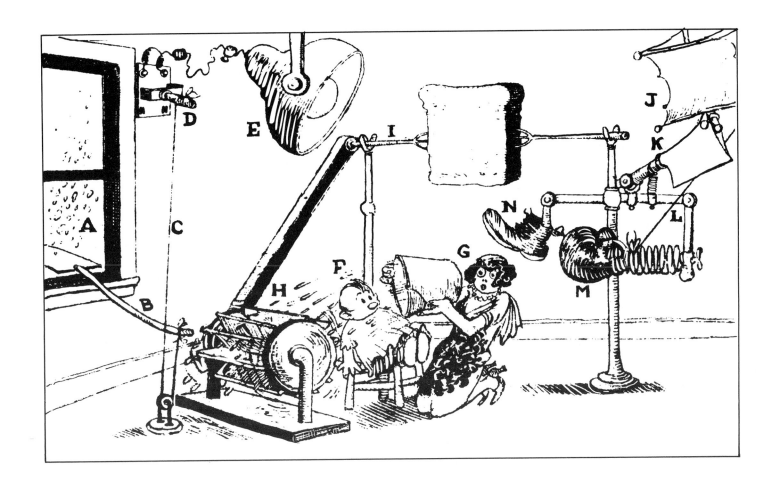

Orange Juice Squeezing Machine

Professor Butts steps into an open elevator shaft and when he lands at the bottom he finds a simple orange squeezing machine. Milkman takes empty milk bottle (**A**), pulling string (**B**) which causes sword (**C**) to sever cord (**D**) and allow guillotine blade (**E**) to drop and cut rope (**F**) which releases battering ram (**G**). Ram bumps against open door (**H**), causing it to close. Grass sickle (**I**) cuts a slice off end of orange (**J**)–at the same time spike (**K**) stabs "prune hawk" (**L**) he opens his mouth to yell in agony, thereby releasing prune and allowing diver's boot (**M**) to drop and step on sleeping octopus (**N**). Octopus awakens in a rage and, seeing diver's face which is painted on orange, attacks it and crushes it with tentacles, thereby causing all the juice in the orange to run into glass (**O**).

Later on you can use the log to build a log cabin where you can raise your son to be President like Abraham Lincoln.

Keeping the Baby Happy While You are Out to the Movies

Professor Butts forgets to leave a building which is being demolished, and when they dig him out of the debris he has an idea for keeping the baby happy while you are out to the movies.

As you go out, door (**A**) pulls cord (**B**) causing tennis racket (**C**) to hit ball (**D**) which swings against roly-poly (**E**), causing it to sway to and fro and pull string (**F**) which works jumping-jack (**G**). Jumping-jack's foot kicks trigger of popgun (**H**) and shoots cork (**I**) against chest of cymbal-playing clown (**J**) who claps his cymbals together and squeezes rubber ball (**K**) which is attached to toy rabbit (**L**), causing it to hop. Zipple pup (**M**), thinking the rabbit is alive, jumps up and down to catch it and jerks cord (**N**) which is attached to hobby horse (**O**), causing it to rock and pull horse reins, (**P**) thereby swinging the cradle which finally puts baby to sleep after an evening of fun.

You will not have to bother doing this after the baby is three. Then he will be inviting his friends in to play poker and drink your gin.

Self-Working Sunshade

Professor Butts is operated on for fallen arches and, while under the ether, thinks of a handy, self-working sunshade.

Shadow of bathing girl (**A**) closely resembles a rabbit. Tortoise (**B**), remembering the fable of the tortoise and the hare, starts to race and pulls string (**C**), opening hook (**D**) which allows Jack-in-the-Box (**E**) to jump against pliers (**F**) and squeeze bulb of eye-dropper (**G**) which drips water on stone (**H**)–as drops of water wear away stone, causing it to become lighter, it rises allowing magnet (**I**) to descend. Magnet attracts steel bar (**J**) which leaves the ground with a sudden jump, pulling cord (**K**), opening door of cupboard (**L**), exposing highly polished pot (**M**). As conceited peacock (**N**) sees his reflection, his vanity prompts her to spread his beautiful tail thereby shielding bather and protecting him from sunburn.–Each morning you can write the peacock a lot of admiring fan letters to make sure he is good and conceited by the time you need him.

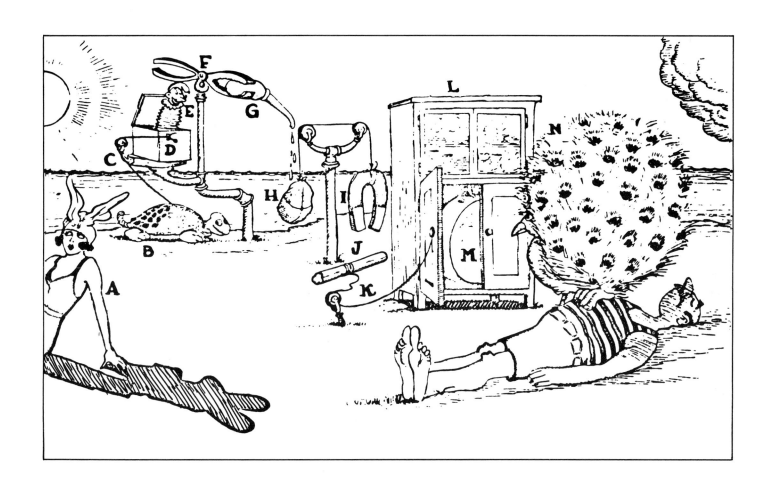

Simple Way to Carve a Turkey

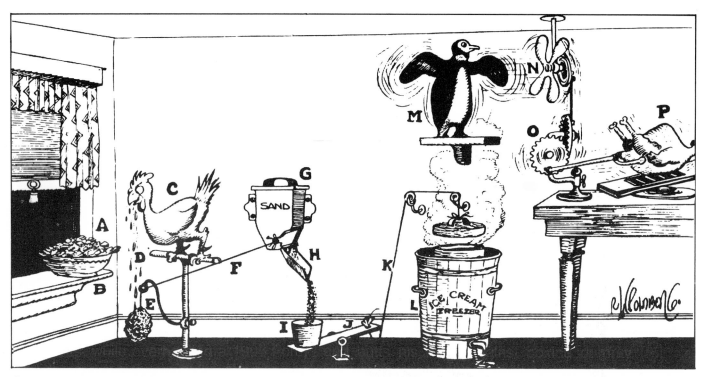

Simple way to carve a turkey. This invention fell off the professor's head with the rest of the dandruff.

Put bowl of chicken salad (**A**) on window sill (**B**) to cool. Rooster (**C**) recognizes his wife in salad and is overcome with grief. His tears (**D**) saturate sponge (**E**), pulling string (**F**) which releases trap door (**G**) and allows sand to run down trough (**H**) into pail (**I**). Weight raises end of see-saw (**J**) which makes cord (**K**) lift cover of ice cream freezer (**L**). Penguin (**M**), feeling chill, thinks he is at the North Pole and flaps wings for joy, thereby fanning propeller (**N**) which revolves and turns cogs (**O**), which in turn cause turkey (**P**) to slide back and forth over cabbage-cutter until it is sliced to a frazzle.–

Don't get discouraged if the turkey gets pretty well messed up. It's a cinch it would have eventually become turkey hash anyway.

Find Your Rubbers

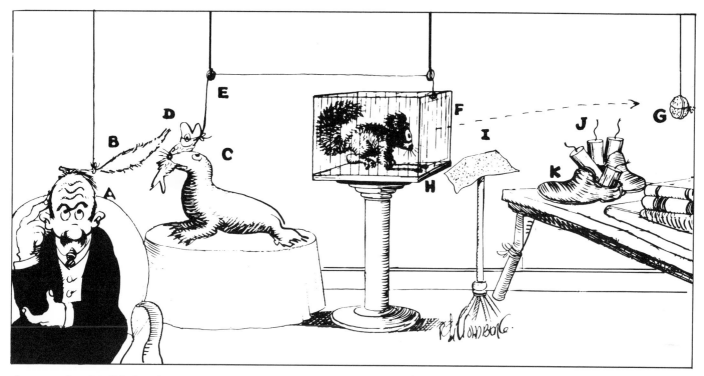

As you try to think where you put your rubbers, your forehead (**A**) wrinkles, causing the top of your head to move and disturb suspended feather (**B**)–feather tickles seal (**C**) which laughs, opens mouth and drops fish (**D**)–weight of fish causes string (**E**) to open door of cage (**F**), releasing squirrel which dives at nut (**G**)–matches (**H**) are tied to squirrel's front paws–as squirrel flies past piece of sandpaper (**I**), matches are lighted and set off fire-crackers (**J**)–noise of explosions shows you immediately where rubbers (**K**) are. If rubbers take fire, squirrel on finding nut is an imitation, breaks down and cries and tears put out flames.

Insure Safety at Railroad Crossing

Professor Butts steals a ride on top of a train, forgets to duck at the entrance of a tunnel, and blurts out an idea to insure safety at railroad crossings.

As commuter (**A**) hears train whistle he thinks he is late and runs across field to make short-cut, scaring out jack-rabbit (**B**) who attracts attention of Giffik Hound (**C**). Hound jumps, pulling string (**D**) which raises end of board (**E**) and pushes handle of squirt gun (**F**) which wets back of duck (**G**). As water rolls off duck's back it runs down through (**H**) onto sponge (**I**). As sponge becomes heavy, extra weight pulls hook (**J**), causing it to release spring (**K**), causing baseball bat (**L**) to hit baseball (**M**) into catcher's glove (**N**) and push box of tacks (**O**) from shelf. As tacks spill on road they puncture tires and force dumb driver to stop, even though he wants to beat speeding train at crossing.

The tire expense is quite an item but tire bills are generally smaller than undertakers' bills.

Self-Scrubbing Bath Brush

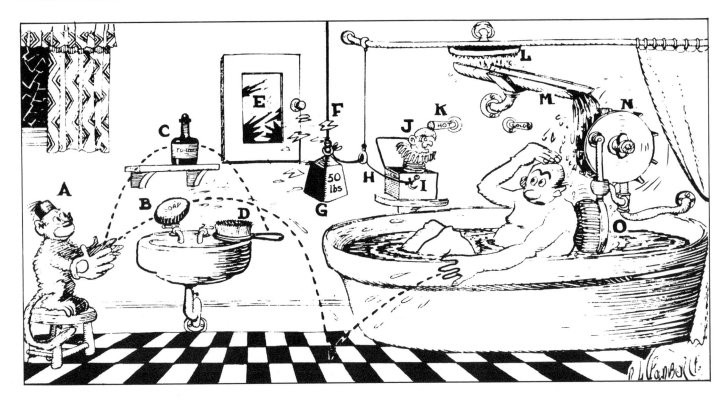

Professor Butts jumps from a plane in a moth-eaten parachute, lands on his head and lives to invent a self-scrubbing bath brush.

Soap slips from bather's hands. Monkey outfielder (**A**) tries to catch it and fumbles. Soap (**B**) hits bottle (**C**) which falls on handle of hair brush, (**D**) causing brush to fly up and smash mirror (**E**). Flying fragments of glass cut cord (**F**), allowing weight (**G**) to drop and pull string (**H**) which opens hook (**I**), releasing Jack-in-the Box (**J**) which jumps up and hits handle (**K**), turning on water in shower (**L**). As water runs down trough (**M**) it falls on mill-wheel (**N**), causing it to revolve and work brush (**O**) up and down on bather's back.

You can rent an organ and keep the monkey busy when you are not taking a bath.

Putting the Cat Out at Night

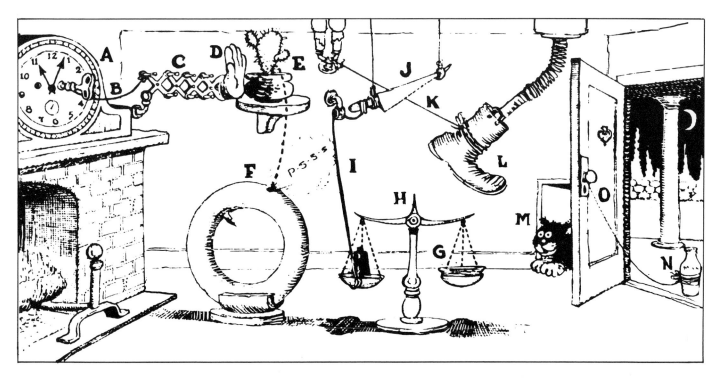

Professor Butts tries to play the xylophone with two sticks of dynamite and when he is picked up three miles away he mumbles incoherently about a simple idea for putting the cat out at night. As you wind clock (**A**) it tightens string (**B**), causing it to extend collapsible hatrack (**C**). Glove (**D**) pushes cactus plant (**E**) from shelf. Cactus needle punctures inner-tube (**F**), causing hissing sound which cat mistakes for someone calling.

As cat approaches she discovers saucer of milk (**G**) standing on scale (**H**) and as she drinks milk weight becomes lighter, causing scale to pull cord (**I**) and draw knife (**J**) across string (**K**), releasing boot (**L**) which pushes cat (**M**) out the door. As cat is pushed out she upsets milk bottle (**N**) which rolls and pulls cord (**O**), closing door. If boot misses cat, then put boot on right foot and kick the cat out yourself.

Sending a Late Stayer Home

Man in restaurant mistakes Professor Butts for a herring, sprinkles pepper on him and he sneezes up an idea for sending a late-stayer home.

At 1 a.m. door of cuckoo clock (**A**) opens, causing string (**B**) to pull trigger of gun (**C**) and shoot cuckoo (**D**), which falls on board (**E**). Weight of cuckoo throws knife (**F**) against sand bag (**G**), cutting hole (**H**) in bag, allowing sand (**I**) to run down on scale (**J**). Cord (**K**) closes shears (**L**) which cut string (**M**), allowing mask (**N**) to descend over victim's head (**O**). Lodge goat (**P**), thinking that late-stayer is being initiated, butts him out into the street.

Don't worry about his hat and coat as he will not need them in the hospital.

Simplified Lawn Sprinkler

A noted surgeon operates on Professor Butts for appendicitis and while unconscious the prof babbles an idea for a simplified lawn sprinkler. When your daughter's beau (**A**) whistles under her window, snake (**B**) mistakes sound for the flute of a snake charmer. As snake comes out of basket (**C**) it frightens frog (**D**) who leaps for safety into bird bath (**E**) and splashes water into pail (**F**), causing rod (**G**) to raise hood (**H**), exposing basket of peanuts (**I**). Squirrel (**J**) plunges for peanuts, thereby revolving platform (**K**). Each time it revolves, knife (**L**) slices onion (**M**). Fumes from onion bring tears to eyes of crocodile (**N**). Speed of revolutions helps scatter the crocodile tears over lawn, thereby watering it.

If your daughter's beau doesn't show up in the first place, then you'll either have to wait for rain or buy a hose.

Self-Opening Umbrella

Professor Butts tries to write a letter on a piece of flypaper and while struggling to release himself, finds an idea for a self-opening umbrella.

Raindrops (**A**) fall on dried prune (**B**), causing it to swell and push against stick (**C**) which forces iron hand (**D**) to rub wheel against flint (**E**) in empty cigar-lighter (**F**). Flying sparks (**G**) ignite candle (**H**) which starts water in kettle (**I**) boiling. Escaping steam (**J**) blows whistle (**K**). Circus monkey (**L**) thinks whistle is master's signal to start act and jumps on trapeze (**M**) which swings and causes edge of knife (**N**) to sever cord (**O**), releasing toy balloon (**P**). As balloon ascends attached string (**Q**) opens door of cage releasing Ikklebirds (**R**) which fly in all directions, causing strings to lift ends of umbrella. If you are hard up and can't afford a new prune for each successive rain storm, stay in the house and wait for the original prune to get old and wrinkled again.

Emptying Ash Trays

Professor Butts trips over a hazard on a miniature golf course and lands on an idea for an automatic device for emptying ash trays.

Bright full moon (**A**) causes love birds (**B**) to become romantic and as they get together their weight causes perch (**C**) to tip and pull string (**D**), which upsets can (**E**) and sprinkles woolen shirt, (**F**) causing it to shrink and draw aside curtain, exposing portrait of wigwag pup's master (**G**). As pup (**H**) sees master's picture he wigwags tail for joy and upsets ash tray (**I**), spilling ashes and smouldering butts into asbestos bag (**J**) attached to sky rocket (**K**). Butt (**L**), passing fuse (**M**), ignites it and causes rocket to shoot out of window, disposing of ashes.

You should always have twenty or thirty high-powered aeroplanes ready to go out and search for the asbestos bag.

Windshield Wiper

Professor Butts swallows his false teeth and coughs up a design for a new windshield wiper.

Weight of rain (**A**) in sponge (**B**) causes string (**C**) to spin fan (**D**). Breeze from fan swings weather vane (**E**) which upsets bag of seeds (**F**) into flower pot (**G**). As seeds grow and bloom, caterpillars (**H**) spin cocoons which naturally become butterflies and fly to flowers, thereby allowing weight of board (**I**) to lower magnet (**J**) which attracts iron bar (**K**), causing string (**L**) to open box (**M**). Soup bone (**N**) drops in front of Zozzle Hound (**O**). He wags tail for joy, wiping rain from windshield.

The big problem is to get the butterflies to hatch before the rain stops. Ask the king of Spain about his. He has plenty of time to figure it out.

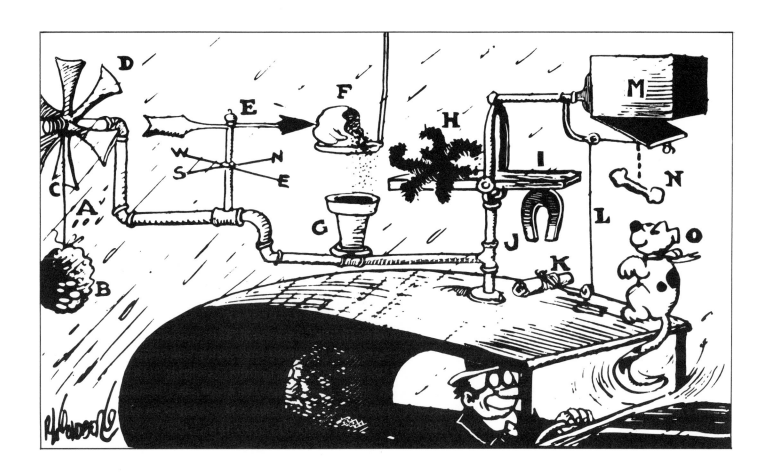

Keeping Screen Doors Closed

Professor Butts makes a parachute jump, forgets to pull the string and wakes up three weeks later with an automatic device for keeping screen doors closed.

Houseflies (**A**), seeing open door, fly on porch. Spider (**B**) descends to catch them and frightens potato-bug (**C**), which jumps from hammer (**D**), allowing it to drop on pancake turner (**E**) which tosses pancake into pan (**F**). Weight of pancake causes pan to tilt and pull cord (**G**) which starts mechanical soldier (**H**) walking. Soldier walks to edge of table and catches his head in noose (**I**), thereby hanging himself. Weight in noose causes string to pull lever and push shoe against bowling ball (**J**), throwing it into hands of circus monkey (**K**) who is expert bowler. Monkey throws ball at bowling pins painted on screen door thereby closing it with a bang.

The monkey is liable to get sore when he discovers that the bowling pins are phony, so it is a good idea to take him to a real bowling alley once in a while just to keep his good will.

Self-Operating Napkin

Professor Butts walks in his sleep, strolls through a cactus field in his bare feet, and screams out an idea for self-operating napkin.

As you raise spoon of soup (**A**) to your mouth it pulls string (**B**), thereby jerking ladle (**C**) which throws cracker (**D**) past parrot (**E**). Parrot jumps after cracker and perch (**F**) tilts, upsetting seeds (**G**) into pail (**H**). Extra weight in pail pulls cord (**I**) which opens and lights automatic cigar lighter (**J**), setting off sky-rocket (**K**) which causes sickle (**L**) to cut string (**M**) and allow pendulum with attached napkin to swing back and forth thereby wiping off your chin.

After the meal, substitute a harmonica for the napkin and you'll be able to entertain the guests with a little music.

Simple Parachute

Professor Butts gets his whiskers caught in a laundry wringer and as he comes out the other end he thinks of an idea for a simple parachute.

As aviator jumps from plane, force of wind opens umbrella (**A**) which pulls cord (**B**) and closes shears (**C**), cutting off corner of feather pillow (**D**). As white feathers (**E**) fly from pillow, penguin (**F**) mistakes them for snow flakes and flaps his wings for joy which draws buck-saw (**G**) back and forth cutting log of wood (**H**). As piece of wood falls into basket (**I**), its weight causes rope (**J**) to pull trigger of gun (**K**) which explodes and shoots lock from cage (**L**), releasing giant Umpha Bird (**M**) which flies and keeps aviator afloat with rope (**N**). Aviator breaks paper bag of corn (**O**), causing corn to fall to ground when bird swoops down to eat corn. Flier unhooks apparatus and walks home.

The biggest problem is where to get the Umpha Bird. Write your Congressman.

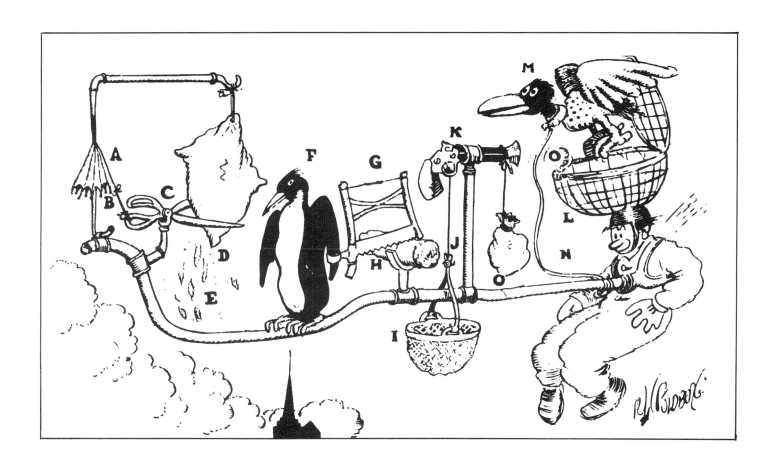

Scientific Barometer

Professor Butts is hit with an angel cake and the angels whisper an idea for a new scientific barometer.

Flash of lightning (**A**) from distant thunder storm sends electrical vibrations (**B**) to magnetic spring (**C**) which contracts and causes knife (**D**) to cut cord (**E**) and release horseshoe (**F**), allowing it to drop on string (**G**) and pull trigger of cannon (**H**) which shoots a hole in wall. Rat (**I**), seeing a new entrance to living room, enters and is caught in trap (**J**) which springs and pulls rope (**K**), raising storm signal flag (**L**). Ex-sailor (**M**), who is a little cuckoo, thinks he is at sea and hauls down sail, (**N**) causing top boom (**O**) to strike against arrow (**P**) and swing it to position, indicating storm.

If you have trouble in finding a nutty sailor, get a sane sailor and drive him crazy by telling him they are going to close up saloons all over the world.

Outboard Motor that Requires No Fuel

Professor Butts tries to fix a leak in the boiler and when he is rescued from drowning he coughs up an idea for an outboard motor that requires no fuel.

As you reach for anchor, button (**A**) snaps loose and hits spigot (**B**), causing beer to run into pail (**C**). Weight pulls cord (**D**), firing shot gun (**E**). Report frightens sea gull (**F**) which flies away and causes ice (**G**) to lower in front of false teeth (**H**). As teeth chatter from cold they bite cord (**I**) in half, allowing pointed tool (**J**) to drop and rip bag of corn (**K**). Corn falls into net (**L**). Weight causes it to snap latch, opening floor of cage (**M**) and dropping duck into shafts (**N**). As duck (**O**) tries to reach corn it swims and causes canoe to move ahead.

If the false teeth keep on chattering you can let them chew your gum to give your own jaws a rest.

105

Picture-Snapping Machine

As you sit on pneumatic cushion (**A**), you force air through tube (**B**) which starts ice boat (**C**), causing lighted cigar butt (**D**) to explode balloon (**E**).

Dictator (**F**), hearing loud report, thinks he's been shot and falls over backward on bulb (**G**), snapping picture!

Mouse Eliminator

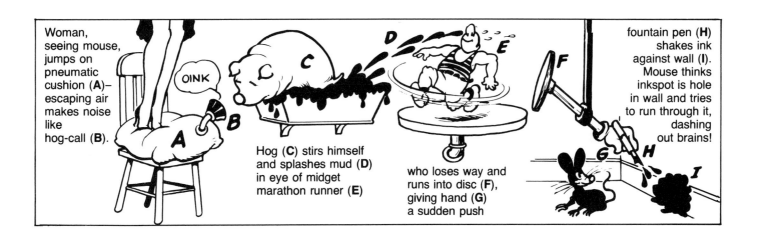

Simple Way to Hitch a Ride

Extinguishing Lighted Cigarette Butts

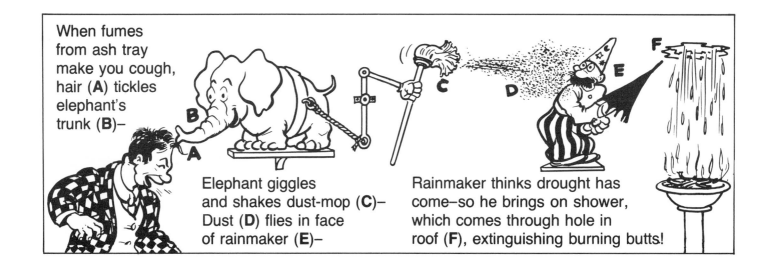

When fumes from ash tray make you cough, hair (**A**) tickles elephant's trunk (**B**)—

Elephant giggles and shakes dust-mop (**C**)— Dust (**D**) flies in face of rainmaker (**E**)—

Rainmaker thinks drought has come—so he brings on shower, which comes through hole in roof (**F**), extinguishing burning butts!

No More Discomfort at Help-Yourself Buffet Suppers

Flattop haircut for balancing fruit

Bow tie with folding trays

Drop-shelf patch pockets

Extension trays from pants pockets

Shirt studs with folding cups for salt and pepper

Special long-distance fork

No More
Gasoline
Problems

Driver opens
trapdoor (**A**)–Monkey (**B**)
reaches for banana (**C**),
upsetting basket
of cotton (**D**)–Ducks (**E**),
mistaking cotton
for snow, think
winter has arrived
and fly south,
pulling car forward.

South
P.S.–These
are vitamin-fed
superducks.

No More Strikes

When worker and boss disagree, their language shocks hear-no-evil monkey (**A**) –Monkey reaches for ear-muffs (**B**), causing cable (**C**) to turn shaft (**D**)– Platform (**E**) revolves, putting worker in boss's place and boss in worker's place–Each sees how tough the other fellow's job is and is glad to call off all future hostilities!

No More Handyman Casualties

When father tries to hang picture, breeze from hammer (**A**) turns pinwheel (**B**), causing hand (**C**) to nudge trained parrot (**D**)–Parrot shouts home address into speaker-system (**E**) which goes direct to city hospital–Father then proceeds to hit thumb, choke on picture wire, fall off ladder and cut self on expensive vase, giving doctor (**F**) plenty of time to get there and save his life.

No More Summer Bugs

Put sponge-headed decoy (**A**) in your bed–Bug (**B**) flies into noose (**C**), upsetting salt seller (**D**) and sprinkling salt on sponge–When bug gets full of salted sponge he becomes very thirsty– He drinks from fountain (**E**), swells up and bursts– Explosion scares off other bugs and you go back to bed.

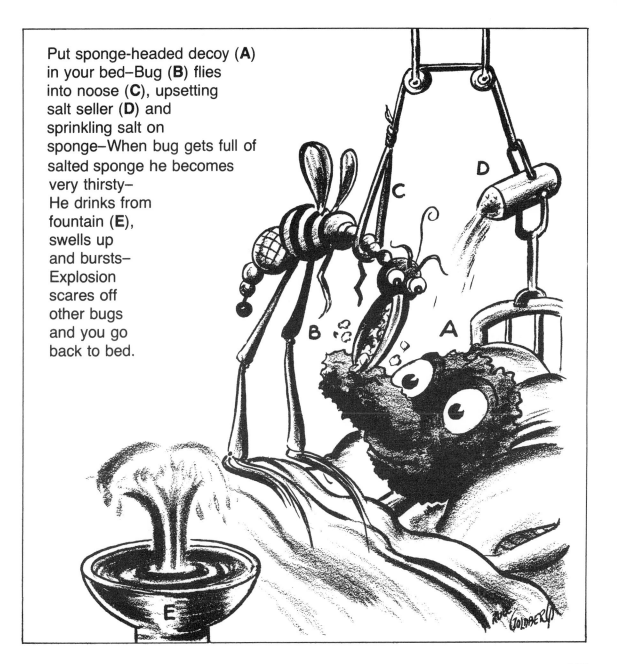

No More Clogging of Bus Entrances

This polite little hint will help people step to the rear and make room for other passengers–This also saves the bus driver's voice for singing in the bathtub.

No More Parking Problems

When you take your car from garage
to go downtown, you kiss your wife goodbye,
moving rod (**A**) and causing Jimmy Durante doll
(**B**) to press switch (**C**) on television set (**D**),
which projects image (**E**), showing impossible
parking conditions on Main Street–
So you put your car back in garage and walk
to work–This not only saves gas and tires
but also gives you a chance to break in
a new pair of shoes.

No More Oversleeping

When sun comes up, magnifying glass (**A**) burns hole in paper bag (**B**), dropping water into ladle (**C**) and lifting gate (**D**), which allows heavy ball (**E**) to roll down chute (**F**)– Rope (**G**) lifts bed (**H**) into vertical position and drops you into your shoes (**I**).

P.S. You can't go back and sneak a few winks because there's no place to lie down!

No More Race Track Losses

Place two dollars in betting machine and pull handle—When money passes through machine your coat is gently lifted and your dough is dropped into your back pocket—After your horse loses, you reach in back pocket for handkerchief to dry your tears and discover you are still even!

PLACE BETS HERE

RUBE GOLDBERG

No More Lost Eyeglasses

When you start looking for glasses, you feel your way around room and your hands (**A**) tilt moose head (**B**), causing antlers (**C**) to knock over pineapple (**D**), lifting top off bird cage (**E**). Hungry canary (**F**) jumps for birdseed in container (**G**), rocking arm (**H**) and ringing bell (**I**), giving location of glasses.

P.S. If pineapples are not in season, a grapefruit will do.

No More Divorces

When wife bounces pitcher (**A**)
off husband's head
it lands in catcher's mitt (**B**),
causing teeter-board (**C**)
to throw midget aerial artist (**D**)
to flying trapeze (**E**)–
Weight on trapeze releases
mink coat (**F**), which
falls on wife's shoulders,
rekindling old love!

No More Fishing Around in Handbags

Each handbag is equipped with cash register and filing cabinet– There is also room for the dog so you can take him along to the movies.

No More Crowded Dance Floors

When floor-hogs crush you against wall, your head squeezes bulb (**A**), expelling laughing gas (**B**), causing hyena (**C**) to vibrate with laughter–Thumb (**D**) presses on sponge (**E**) and water (**F**) turns water wheel (**G**), causing cord (**H**) to pull down shade (**I**), exposing sign reading small pox, and clearing floor for your pleasure.

No More Inferiority Complex for Short Men

When he tips hat to girl
he turns on steam in powerhouse (**A**),
causing crane (**B**) to lift
him into tall trousers
giving him desired height
to be taken seriously as a wolf.

No More Unlucky Fisherman

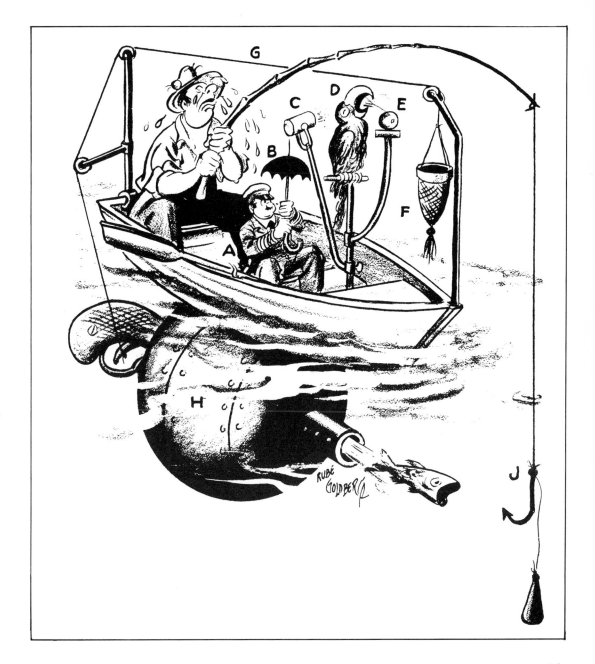

After fishing all day without a bite, you shed tears of chagrin–Midget rowboat captain (**A**), thinking it is raining, lifts umbrella (**B**), upsetting can of sneeze-powder (**C**)–Parrot (**D**) sneezes, blowing pool ball (**E**) into pocket (**F**)–String (**G**) pulls trigger of attached steel aquarium (**H**), shooting fish (**I**) on to hook (**J**)–You can catch a nice brook trout without taking an expensive trip to the mountains and getting eaten up by mosquitoes.

Automatic Woman's Hat Remover at Movies

As you burn with indignation, fumes (**A**) melt wax (**B**), causing scissors (**C**) to cut string (**D**)–Weight (**E**) falls and pulls out stick (**F**), allowing alligator (**G**) to bite off hat (**H**), clearing visibility.

P.S. Usher immediately removes apparatus so man in back of you can see, too.

Every Woman to Have a Perfect Figure

She sits down to eat in scale (**A**)–As weight increases, magnet (**B**) moves toward small steel bar (**C**), picking it up and tilting groove (**D**)–Golf ball (**E**) drops on ant-hill (**F**)–Midget beginner (**G**) takes swing at ball, misses it and knocks chunk out of ant-hill, scattering ants–Anteater (**H**) goes after ants, moving table away from hungry young lady, allowing her to preserve her beautiful figure.

Index

Typewriter, 57

U
Umbrella, 92

V
Vest, 3

W
Washing dishes, 51
Weight reducing, 1, 125
Whipped cream, 62
Wife, 63
Window, 25, 52
Windshield wiper, 95